AUBREY BURL

PREHISTORIC
ASTRONOMY
AND RITUAL

SHIRE ARCHAEOLOGY

Cover illustration
Stonehenge
(Photograph: Professor Owen Gingerich)

Published by
SHIRE PUBLICATIONS LTD
Cromwell House, Church Street, Princes Risborough,
Aylesbury, Bucks, HP17 9AJ, UK.

Series Editor: James Dyer

ISBN 0 85263 621 0

First published 1983; reprinted.

Set in 12 point Times roman and printed in Great Britain by
C. I. Thomas & Sons (Haverfordwest) Ltd,
Merlins Bridge, Haverfordwest.

Contents

4

List of illustrations

1
Introduction

There are two questions about prehistoric astronomy in the British Isles. The first is whether it ever existed, whether people did align some of their burial places and shrines on the risings and settings of the sun and moon or whether this is just an illusion created by mistaken interpretations of Stonehenge and other monuments. The second question is more subtle. If prehistoric astronomy did exist, what was it used for? Were there astronomer-priests scientifically studying the heavens or were the alignments for other purposes, for the dead and for the spirits of the Other-World?

It will be a long time before these questions are answered but already it is possible to show what people have thought about these problems and how some solutions are appearing. The reading list at the end of the book gives a glimpse of the number of books and articles that have been written. In 1923 Rear-Admiral Boyle Somerville, a pioneer of megalithic astronomy, wrote: 'The occurrence of orientation in prehistoric structures has long been noticed. It has not, however, received from investigators much more than a passing comment.'

This is no longer true. Archaeologists are recognising that orientation is as important as architecture and artefacts to anyone examining the ritual centres of prehistory. This book demonstrates how far we have gone in these studies, largely owing to the stimulus of scholars such as Gerald Hawkins and Alexander Thom.

Because the radiocarbon method is now known to produce prehistoric 'dates' which are too young these have been converted into real years. Thus a C-14 'date' of 1200 ± 150 bc for the stone circle at Sandy Road, Scone, becomes 1495 BC. Such conversions bring the dates into line with the accurate astronomical chronology of the sun, moon and stars.

I am grateful to my many colleagues, particularly Richard Atkinson, Gerald Hawkins, Douglas Heggie, Euan MacKie, Jon Patrick, Clive Ruggles, and Alexander Thom and his son, Archie, who by their conversations, questions and, above all, by their fieldwork have helped me to a better understanding of the mysteries of archaeoastronomy.

Plate 1. The row at Ballochroy looking to the north-west and the island of Jura. (Photograph: Crown Copyright, Ancient Monuments Record, Edinburgh.)

Plate 2. Ballochroy from the north. The cist is on the right.

2
The puzzle of Ballochroy

There are many arguments about what the sun and moon meant to prehistoric people in the British Isles. We have only to look at the famous 'observatory' at Ballochroy to see how many ideas there are about ancient astronomy and how difficult they are to prove.

The western road down the coast of the Kintyre peninsula in Argyll is one of the loveliest in Britain. As it turns and curves alongside the rock-scattered shore it touches black tumbles of boulders hung with fingers of seaweed, stones half-sunk in pools and, beyond them, the dapples of shingle and sand that slope down to the Sound of Jura. To the west, miles across the sea, is the island of Jura itself, its mountains dark and undulating. But to the east of the road the land rises. Here man has cultivated the old raised beaches that climb in broad steps on the hills forming the peninsula's spine. On one of these terraces a few miles south of Tarbert's fishing harbour are the megaliths of Ballochroy.

The three stones that stand in line here have been called the most impressive prehistoric observatory in Britain. These are not boulders but tall slabs, their broad faces set across the row like the beginnings of a house of cards. The shortest stone is at the north-east and from it, looking down the row, one sees a small cist by the field wall, a tree-covered ridge and then, far away to the south-west, the tiny island of Cara. If one then turned to the right, looking through the row instead of down it, and sighted north-westwards along the broad flat faces of the stones, one would find the humped Paps of Jura neatly framed between the slabs.

These views have excited astronomers because the northeast-southwest line of the row and the southeast-northwest axis of the slabs provide alignments on not one but two astronomical events, the midwinter and midsummer sunsets. That such a combination should occur by chance seems unlikely and Ballochroy has been acclaimed as an ideal observatory for astronomer-priests. Alexander Thom has described how the central stone points exactly to the most northerly peak of the Paps where the midsummer setting sun would graze the slope. Six months later an observer looking south-westwards would see the midwinter sun setting against Cara Island. It is not surprising that astronomers such as Gerald Hawkins have thought that Ballochroy is 'an ingeniously neat combination of site selection and astronomical knowledge'. As though to confirm this, only 6 miles (10

Plate 3. William Stukeley's sketch of Ballochroy, copied from Edward Lhuyd, showing the cairn in AD 1700.

km) down the coast at Beacharra the tallest stone on the peninsula is said to indicate the most northerly setting of the moon behind Jura's skyline.

Yet although the evidence seems convincing there are just as good reasons for believing that Ballochroy never was an observatory. The alignment to Cara Island is not very precise. Nor could an observer have seen the sunset there because a huge cairn 40 yards (37 m) away from the stones would have blocked his view. It was completely removed years ago when the field walls were built, leaving the cist exposed, but the name of Ballochroy, *baile-cruach* or 'farm by the mound', shows how conspicuous this cairn once was. The nearby farm, Cairnbeg, 'the little cairn', still has a mound 10 feet (3 m) high. This suggests that Ballochroy's cairn was even bigger and when the antiquarian Edward Lhuyd saw it in 1700 he called it 'Karn mor', the great cairn. His rough sketch shows how it would have obscured any sightline towards Cara.

This does not mean that the people who put up the stones were unaware of the midwinter setting sun. To the contrary, they probably aligned the stones on it as part of the rituals that took place when someone's cremated bones were placed in the cist. But when the funerary ceremonies were over the cairn was heaped up, as monstrous as the surviving mound at Machrihanish 20 miles (32 km) to the south, which is 100 feet (31 m) across, 15 feet (4.6 m) high, and covered a cist like that at Ballochroy. There were standing stones here also.

Nevertheless, even if the south-west alignment at Ballochroy were for the dead this would not explain the very precise and unobscured sightline towards the midsummer sunset at the north-west. This, one would think, had to be intentional. Ironically, it is quite as likely to have been accidental.

Much of the Kintyre peninsula is composed of mica schists which split tidily into thin, broad-faced slabs. It was these local stones that were used at Ballochroy and it is here that geology coincides with astronomy. At that latitude the alignments to midwinter and midsummer sunsets form a right-angle. The decision to have the broad faces of the stones looking to the south-west meant that each slab had to be set up on a southeast-northwest axis at 90 degrees to the row.

Fig. 1. Plan of the row and cist at Ballochroy showing where the great cairn once stood.

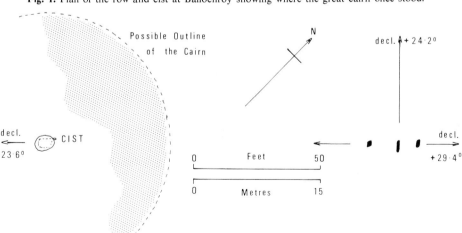

Inevitably each stone was 'aligned' on the midsummer sunset (fig. 1).

It is reasonable to assume that if the builders had been interested in this they would have taken great care to line up all the stones on the sunset. As it is, only the central alignment is accurate. The others are not and this suggests that the midsummer orientation at Ballochroy is merely a consequence of the latitude.

Similar coincidences can be found elsewhere. In the Orkneys midsummer sunrise at 39 degrees from north and the minor southern moonrise at 128 degrees happen virtually at right-angles to each other. Far to the south in Wiltshire the alignments to midsummer sunrise at 51 degrees and to the major northern setting of the moon at 321 degrees form an angle of 90 degrees as seen from the centre of Stonehenge. This has prompted claims that the rectangle of the Four Station stones there was purposely constructed to record these events. Other considerations, however, suggest that the rectangle is as much the result of chance as the two sunset lines at Ballochroy.

These facts do not disprove the theory that Ballochroy was an observatory but they do provide alternative explanations. Clearly, it would be unwise for any archaeo-astronomer to ignore possible coincidences, a danger that may be overcome by examining not one but a group of related sites. It is known that there are other three-stone rows like Ballochroy, such as the line of rounded boulders at Torhousekie in Wigtownshire which is oriented towards midwinter sunset but which does not possess an additional midsummer sightline. The existence of comparable structures with only single alignments must weaken the dual-line interpretation of Ballochroy.

There is yet another mystery. Although little commented on, there is a third alignment along the row towards the north-east, which, in the words of Gerald Hawkins, 'points along an elevated horizon towards the extreme northerly position of the moon'. This is true but one wonders if it mattered. The row does point to where the northern moon rises behind a steep hillside. The central stone does line up with midsummer sunset. Even if they knew these things the builders may have been quite uninterested in them, indifferent to anything except the midwinter sunset and the funerary rites around the cist.

In our enthusiasm to discover how prehistoric observatories worked we may be overlooking what prehistoric people thought. It is important to realise that because there is an alignment it does not follow that it was astronomical. There are many instances of monuments with orientations that can never have been related to any celestial event. From the evidence of societies in other parts of the world it is feasible that such sites were set out to face some natural feature or even another monument. Hills or rivers or valleys may have been deemed sacred or connected with an ancestor or some legendary deed. Only when an alignment is very precise and defined by man-made structures or when it is consistently repeated in a group of similar sites should it be accepted as astronomical.

It is dangerously easy to impose our own ideas on the prehistoric cairns and stones that we study and to distort them into our image. In our own scientific age our interpretations tend to be scientific and we are inclined to attribute significance to every alignment that we discover. The beliefs of earlier workers also reflected the attitudes and prejudices of their times. All researchers are affected by the opinions of the age they live in as the changing ideas about the stone circle and rows at Callanish demonstrate.

Plate 4 *(above)*. Callanish from the south. The ruined passage-grave lies between the tall centre stone and the circle-stones to its right. (Photograph: Derek Simpson.)

Plate 5 *(left)*. Stukeley's sketch of the 'Celtic temple' of Callanish.

3
Early workers at Callanish

It is interesting to see how the belief that prehistoric people were scientists and astronomers developed. The story of Callanish in the Outer Hebrides shows how this slowly came about. Over the ages this marvellous stone circle has undergone a steady transformation from enchanted ring to megalithic observatory and because all the famous researchers from William Stukeley to Alexander Thom have taken part in the process the history of this site is a good example of Jacquetta Hawkes's sceptical words that 'every age gets the Stonehenge it deserves — or desires'.

The circle is not a big one, only 40 feet (12 m) across, but it is built of tall, scrawny stones with an even taller stone near the centre at the back of a devastated and midget passage-grave. Three rows of stones and an avenue lead up to the ring like the arms of a Celtic cross. It is a unique design and the challenge of its radiating lines has been met earnestly by astronomers.

When this 'Stonehenge of the North' was first described by John Morisone around 1680 he thought the stones were simply men 'converted into stone by ane Inchanter' and set up in a ring 'for devotione'. A few years later Martin Martin also said it was a temple built 'in the time of Heathenisme' but by 1720, convinced that sun-worshipping druids had erected it, John Toland wrote that 'this temple stands astronomically . . . dedicated principally to the sun'.

This was the first suggestion that Callanish was more than a rough ring of unworked stones heaved upright by savages for their atrocious rites and it was the beginning of a tendency to regard it as a piece of elegant engineering. In 1743 William Stukeley, also certain of the abilities of the druids, added mathematical exactness to the ring by writing in his *Abury* that 'the circle is 20 cubits in diameter'. He believed, quite wrongly, that the cubit was an exact druidical measure of 20.8 inches (528 mm).

By 1808 Thomas Headrick, an antiquarian writing in the mechanically minded time of the industrial revolution, said he was satisfied that the circle was laid out to the cardinal points of north, east, south and west to mark 'the rising of the sun, moon and stars, the seasons of the year, and even the hours or divisions of the day'. He had turned Callanish into the megalithic equivalent of an orrery, a type of planetarium perfected by Rittenhouse in 1770 just before Headrick's time.

Daniel Wilson, writing in the mid nineteenth century, called Callanish 'a memorial of primitive astronomical knowledge' but added that it was connected 'with native rites of worship in prehistoric times'. Hardly more than a century ago, therefore, the circle was still thought of mainly as a temple for druidical sacrifice, albeit with some astronomical lines built into it.

This equable mixture of ritual and astronomy might have been acceptable in the religious-cum-scientific atmosphere of Victorian times but by the early twentieth century the astronomy became dominant. Sir Norman Lockyer, Director of the Solar Physics Observatory, was dissatisfied with the imprecision of the so-called cardinal alignments. Analysing a plan of Callanish, he deduced that the east row pointed accurately to the rising of the Pleiades in 1330 BC and that the avenue to the NNE indicated the rising of the bright star Capella in 1720 BC.

Rear-Admiral Boyle Somerville made his own survey of Callanish in 1909. From it he calculated that the avenue was directed to Capella in 1800 BC, the east row to the Pleiades in 1750 BC, the south row ran exactly to the meridian, and the west row was aligned on the equinoctial sunsets of March and September. Because some of the circle stones obstructed these delicate sightlines they must, he considered, have been put up by later people 'with the intention of effacing the worship . . . of the dead with the Sun, Moon and stars'.

By the 1960s a computer enabled Gerald Hawkins to discover ten good alignments on the sun and moon at their extremes and another on the moon when it was highest at the south. 'The astronomical alignments are indisputable', he wrote in *Stonehenge Decoded* and pointed out that in that latitude the southern full moon only just rose above the horizon, making its low path across the sky very dramatic.

Ever more rapidly Callanish was losing its rôle as a ritual temple. Increasingly science and astronomy were replacing ceremony and sacrifice. To Alexander Thom in 1967 the ring was a Type A Flattened Circle with diameters of 16 by $14\frac{1}{2}$ of his Megalithic Yards of 2.72 feet (0.829 m). The avenue was 11 Megalithic Yards (29 feet 11 inches or 9.1 m) wide. The southern row was a wonder of exactness, correct to within 0.1 degree of a true north-south line, its precision obtained by the sophisticated bisection of the angle between the east and west elongation of a circumpolar star. Like Somerville, Thom thought the western row was equinoctial and that the avenue was aligned on Capella around 1790 BC. The east row, however, was more probably aimed at the rising of Altair in 1760 BC. He added that 'there is only one obvious explanation of the skew construction at Callanish and that is that the alignments were for astronomical purposes'.

Such speculations are fascinating and stimulating but some of the astronomical work may have been misdirected. Although very few people would doubt that there were sightlines at Callanish these may not have been as exact, or as important, as some of these studies suggest.

The astronomical dates of the rows, for instance, are almost certainly wrong because, from the evidence of Beaker pottery found at the site, Callanish was probably put up around 2400 BC, several centuries earlier than the suggested stellar alignments. From this it follows that the builders could not have aligned the rows on Capella, Altair or the Pleiades because in 2400 BC these were all rising a long way on the horizon from their positions in 1800 BC.

The hypothetical alignments could never have existed and, whatever the reason for their erection, the rows were not starlines. Instead, they may have had functions different from those proposed by astronomers. Possibly the earlier ideas that Callanish was a temple rather than an observatory were more realistic. To test this, one would have to know what part the sun and moon played in the lives of prehistoric people.

4
Sun, moon and prehistoric people

In the twentieth century most eight-year-old children in Britain have learned that the sun rises in the east and sets in the west. Five thousand years ago similar children would have known this was wrong. On countless long summer days they saw the sun rise at the north-east and set at the north-west. They knew that three moons later the slowly shifting sun was rising at the east and that by midwinter it rose far down the chilled skyline at the south-east, only to set a few hours later at the south-west.

In the twentieth century a sixteen-year-old would probably know why this was so. It is unlikely that a bronze age adolescent understood the causes of what happened on the horizon. A modern youth could talk of the earth's tilt, its daily rotation and its annual orbit around the sun. A prehistoric youth would know that there was daylight and darkness, warmth and cold, growing crops and lifeless soil.

This book is less concerned with the mechanics of the solar and lunar cycles than with the double problem of whether ancient societies aligned their ritual monuments on these events and with the methods by which we try to prove this. Why people should want to orientate a chambered tomb or a stone row towards the sun or moon is a question that may never be fully answered but although we may never know what prehistoric people thought about the sun and moon we do know what they saw because the movements of these bodies have scarcely changed in the past five thousand years. By contrast the positions of the stars are very different now from what they were in prehistoric times but as there is little evidence for stellar alignments in the British Isles we can disregard this complication.

In neolithic and bronze age times man would have noticed how the sun or moon moved day by day along the horizon. The skyline would have been familiar to a person living in the countryside and he would see that the rising and setting positions slowly changed in the course of a year. From the inherited lore of his forefathers he would learn that although it was easy to predict where the sun would be from year to year the moon was less simple to anticipate.

Because early prehistoric art in the British Isles was not representational we have no pictures or carvings to tell us whether people believed that the earth went round the sun, or the sun around the earth, whether the sun was drawn by oxen, or floated in a heavenly sea, or was a god who awakened to peer down on earth each day. We can only record what a prehistoric observer would have seen.

He would have noticed that the sun never rose farther up the skyline than the north-east and that when it was there the daylight lasted longer, the weather was warmer and the trees were in leaf. For three or four days the sun appeared at the same spot, its 'standstill' or solstice, and then day after day it rose a little southwards until after six darkening months it reached its extreme winter solstice position at the south-east on 21st December. Man would soon associate the midsummer solstice with light and warmth and the south-east solstice with darkness and cold. The sun provided him with a helpful calendar to mark the seasons despite the disadvantage that one could not look at it directly.

Although few people were aware of it, the solstitial positions of the sun differed according to the latitude. In northern Britain the winter days were shorter and summer days longer than in the south. At Stonehenge daylight on midsummer's day lasted some sixteen and a half hours but at Ballochroy 300 miles (480 km) to the north, there was an extra hour of light because the sun rose and set nearer to the north in that latitude. Table 1 shows how the *azimuths* (the compass bearings clockwise from true north) varied in Britain.

Table 1. Sunrises and sunsets in southern, central and northern Britain.

latitude		*midsummer* (21st June)		*equinoxes* (21st March and 23rd September)		*midwinter* (21st December)	
		rise	*set*	*rise*	*set*	*rise*	*set*
50°	Land's End	51°	309°	90°	270°	129°	231°
55°	SW Scotland	45°	315°	90°	270°	135°	225°
60°	Shetlands	35°	325°	90°	270°	145°	215°

In consequence, investigators have to know the latitude of the monuments they study. Luckily, Ordnance Survey maps provide these in their margins. An azimuth by itself offers only the crudest indication of a solar or lunar event.

Halfway up Britain, at latitude 55 degrees, the sun's risings and settings change greatly from summer to winter, as table 2 shows. These azimuths would be different in another latitude. Outside the north-east entrance of Stonehenge, the Heel Stone outlier, with an azimuth of 51 degrees, stands just about in line with the midsummer sunrise. Had Stonehenge been erected in the Orkneys the midsummer sun would

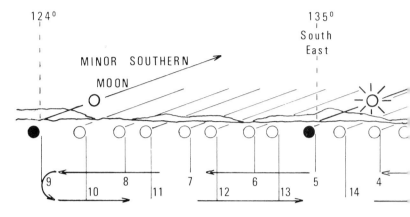

Fig. 2. Annual extreme risings of the southern full moon over the 18.61 year lunar cycle. The south-east horizon at latitude 55 degrees north. The extreme rising positions of the sun and moon are shown as solid black rings. Notice how hills affect the places where sunrise and moonrise appear on the skyline.

have risen at about 38 degrees east of north and the Heel Stone would have been put up over 50 feet (15 m) closer to the north.

Table 2. The monthly rising and setting positions of the sun at latitude 55 degrees, central Britain.

month	sunrise	sunset	hours of daylight
21st June	45°	315°	$17\frac{1}{4}$
21st July	52°	308°	$16\frac{1}{4}$
21st August	69°	291°	$14\frac{1}{4}$
21st September	90°	270°	12
21st October	111°	249°	$9\frac{3}{4}$
21st November	128°	232°	$7\frac{3}{4}$
21st December	135°	225°	$6\frac{3}{4}$

The sun is simple, the moon is complex. The place where it rises moves along the horizon just as the sun does but whereas the sun takes a year to complete its northeast-southeast-northeast cycle the moon takes only a month, the time it takes to circle the earth. Its risings and settings move swiftly from one extreme to the other in a fortnight, waxing and waning from full moon to crescent to invisibility when it is 'new'. Sometimes it rises in daylight so that when darkness comes it can be high in the sky. Another difficulty in observing it is that there can be a full moon only when it is opposite the sun, which provides its light. At midwinter, when the sun is at the south, a full moon would be at the north. When the sun, moon and Earth are more or less in line it is called the *syzygy*. The moon is new and in darkness

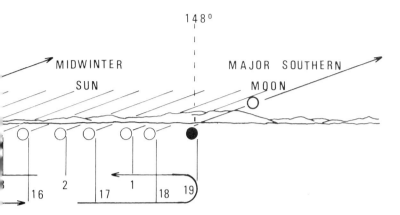

when it is between the sun and the earth. It is full and bright when it is on the far side of the earth from the sun.

The rapidity of the moon's movements, its changing shape and its periodic disappearance must have intrigued, perhaps awed prehistoric people. Because it was a body easily seen at night and capable of being looked at with the naked eye some alignments were directed towards it. It has, however, a third and considerable handicap.

Its extreme positions both at north and south expand and contract over a period of 18.61 years. At latitude 55 degrees an observer one year would see the midsummer full moon rise at its southernmost extreme around 148 degrees. Unlike the sun's, however, this standstill point was not unalterable. Instead, in succeeding years the moon rose farther and farther from 148 degrees until after nine years it reached only as far south as 124 degrees, its minor standstill. In that year the full moon would rise there at midsummer, setting at 236 degrees, and at midwinter it would rise at 56 degrees and set at 304 degrees. Then it would begin its slow return to its major standstill when its midsummer and midwinter arcs were from 148 degrees to 212 degrees and from 32 degrees to 328 degrees.

So involved is this lunar cycle, together with the added confusions of the rapid monthly movement and frequent daylight ascents, that it would have taken years of observations, perhaps even several generations, for prehistoric people to be certain that they had located the standstills accurately.

Figure 2 shows what our imaginary observer would have seen on the south-eastern horizon at his latitude of 55 degrees. The sun rises at the winter solstice at 135 degrees. The moon at its major standstill rises at 148 degrees. Each succeeding year it will rise farther from the south until it reaches the minor standstill at 124 degrees. Similar diagrams could be drawn for the north-eastern, north-western and south-western skylines.

The possible effects of forests and cloudy skies upon this idealised model will be considered later but what can no longer be ignored are the ridges and humps of the horizon. If the skyline happened to be level with a prehistoric site then there is little problem. Sadly, this is rare. Generally there is a hill or looming moor beyond the site and the closer it is the more difference it will make.

The sun and moon do not climb vertically into the sky but rise in graceful angles to the horizon. If their ascents were hidden for a while behind a wide and high mountain ridge the azimuths of where they first appeared on the skyline would be affected. At latitude 55 degrees if there were a hill five miles (8 km) away and 1,000 feet (305 m) above the observer the midwinter sunrise there at 135 degrees would be concealed and the sun would not become visible until it cleared the hill at about 140 degrees.

Account must therefore be taken not only of the latitude of a site and the azimuth of any possible alignment but also of the altitude of the horizon. This combination of latitude, azimuth and horizon produces the *declination* of a celestial object. In 3000 BC the sun's declination at the midsummer solstice was + 24.027 degrees and at midwinter − 24.027 degrees. The moon at its major standstills had declinations of + or − 29.177 degrees, and at its minor standstills + or − 18.887 degrees. For practical purposes these declinations have remained constant because over the next thousand years they changed by less than one-tenth of a degree.

Declination is calculated by the formula:

$$\sin d = (\sin l \times \sin h) + (\cos l \times \cos h \times \cos az)$$

where d = declination, l = latitude, h = horizon height, and az = azimuth. Before the days of pocket calculators this was somewhat forbidding but today it is worked out very simply.

The effects of other important but relatively minor matters such as refraction and parallax need not be discussed here. Anyone with more than a general interest in archaeo-astronomy should refer to Alexander Thom's *Megalithic Sites in Britain*, where such refinements are discussed and where tables are given for their solution.

Most readers will be more interested in why people in prehistoric Britain were concerned with the movements of the sun and moon, what sort of astronomical monuments they built, and when these activities first began.

5
The primitive phase
4000 to 3000 BC

The earliest investigators of prehistoric astronomy paid most attention to stone circles. More recent workers have included rows of stones in their researches. Perhaps because of this concentration on settings of standing stones it is still not generally realised that many neolithic tombs, some over a thousand years older than the first stone circles, also were planned to face the sun or moon.

For a long time archaeologists have known that the axis of a normal long barrow in Britain was so arranged that the mound's wider, higher end covering the burials nearly always pointed somewhere between NNE and SSE. This is true also of megalithic tombs with stone-lined chambers. The earliest were probably quite small, simple family vaults but whether the chamber stood at the end of a long cairn, such as Lochhill in Dumfries-shire, erected around 3900 BC, or at the centre of a round passage-grave, like those built some time later at Knowth in County Meath, there was an accepted direction for the entrance to face.

Every region had its own tradition (fig. 3). Almost all these early tombs looked eastwards but whereas the long cairns in the Cotswolds had entrances lying anywhere between north-east and south-east those of south-western Scotland, very similar in their architecture to the Wessex barrows, had a much narrower range between NNE and ENE. In Brittany the majority of the entrances clustered around the south-east.

Commonsense suggests that these restricted arcs resulted from the tomb builders aligning their entrances on some astronomical event. Somerville believed that the Hebridean passage-grave of Barpa Langass was aligned on the midwinter sunset. West Kennet in Wiltshire looks towards the equinoctial sunrise. Round Camster in Caithness with its long, east-facing passage may also have been oriented on the equinoctial sun rising over the nearby Hill of Yarrows.

Other societies are known to have linked death with the sun and moon. Neolithic people may have thought these were the homes of ancestors or that their rays would reanimate the souls of the dead. The American painter George Catlin described how Mandan Indians in Dakota would expose a corpse on a high scaffold 'with its feet

Plate 6. Round Camster passage-grave, Caithness, from the east. (Photograph: Derek Simpson.)

carefully presented towards the rising sun'. Navajo Indians believed that death was a companion of the sun and moon, and in the Pacific the Caroline Islanders said their ancestors died again when the moon waned but revived on its re-emergence as a crescent in the sky.

Beliefs such as these may have led to the earliest known alignments in the British Isles, rough orientations whose accuracy was affected by many other considerations. Some regions may have been content to set a tomb in line with sunrise at any time of the year. Others may have believed that only midwinter or midsummer orientations were effective. It is, in any case, unlikely that many of these sightlines were precise. The lie of the land, the quality of the building stone, the skill of the builders, the need to make the tomb conspicuous, all may have influenced the direction of the passage. Moreover, because this passage had to be wide enough to admit a person dragging a corpse or clutching a bundle of skeletal bones the arc of vision from the chamber could be very broad. Such coarse orientations may have satisfied the spiritual needs of a neolithic family but they cannot delight the mind of an archaeo-astronomer looking for indisputable alignments.

To his further discomfiture some tombs may have had no astronomical significance at all. Several cairns of the Carrowkeel cemetery in County Sligo were laid out to look not towards the northern moonset but the gigantic mound of Maeve's Cairn on

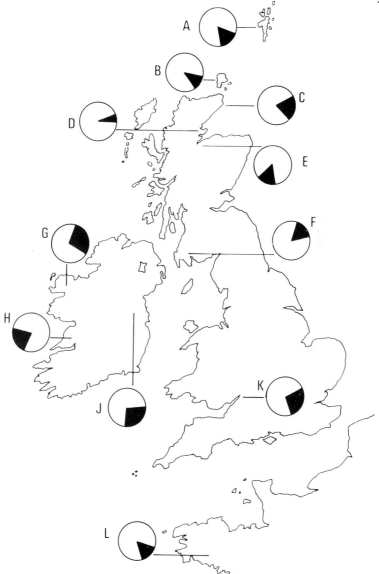

Fig. 3. The azimuths of some groups of chambered tombs. (A) Shetland heel-shaped cairns; (B) Orkney stalled cairns; (C) Camster tombs, Caithness; (D) Camster tombs, Ross and Cromarty; (E) Clava Cairns; (F) Clyde long mounds; (G) Court-Cairns, County Mayo; (H) wedge-graves; (J) Boyne passage-graves; (K) Cotswold-Severn long mounds; (L) passage-graves, Brittany.

Plate 7. La-Roche-aux-Fées, Brittany, from the east. (Photograph: Alex Gibson.)

Knocknarea mountain several miles to the north-west. The west-facing passage-grave of Wideford Hill on Orkney is less likely to have been aligned on the equinoctial sunset than upon the probably earlier tomb of Cuween at the other side of a wide fertile plain. One can detect such exceptions because they are exactly that, exceptions to the rule which can be recognised only when whole groups of similar sites are studied.

As well as the alignments themselves there are other clues to the astronomical interests of neolithic people. Carvings, apparently of suns, in some Irish passage-graves support the idea of a prehistoric association between the dead and the sky and Martin Brennan believes he has identified a lunar calendar engraved on one of the kerbstones at Knowth in the Boyne valley.

Legends also may help in our search because they too hint at solar or lunar rituals. In Somerset the capstone of the Waterstone long mound is supposed to dance on midsummer's day whenever the moon is full. The massive megalithic gallery-grave of La-Roche-aux-Fées in Brittany is reputedly in line with the southern moonrise. The lack of finds in this so-called tomb and the tradition of courting couples counting the stones on the night of the new moon implies that this imposing monument may have been a shrine rather than a grave, a place where neolithic families held their ceremonies when the moon was bright.

Plate 8. The roofbox and its carved lintel above the entrance to Newgrange passage-grave, County Meath. (Photograph: M. J. O'Kelly.)

As the centuries of the new stone age passed the tombs gradually lost their rôle as simple family burial places and became ossuaries in which ancestral bones and skulls were used by the living in rites of fertility and magic. By the end of the fourth millennium newly built mounds such as Newgrange in County Meath, dated to about 3200 BC, were really grandiose temples, huge structures for the use of large assemblies. In them the alignments were more nicely defined.

Above the lintelled entrance of Newgrange is a narrow, stone-slabbed aperture like a giant-sized letterbox. Such a superfluous feature seemed inexplicable. Legend, however, had it that sunlight somehow penetrated the blocked-up passage and illuminated a triple spiral carved in the dark chamber at the heart of the cairn. Experiments showed that for a few days around the winter solstice the rising sun shone through the gap of the 'roofbox', its rays reaching down the passage to the three chambers where the bones of the dead had rested. So well planned was this alignment and so ideal was the roofbox that this almost certainly was its intended purpose but had the alignment been for a living observer the aperture would have been unnecessary because the passage would not have been blocked. It should be noticed, though, that the roofbox was usually closed with two quartz stones that were pushed aside at midwinter. Somebody outside the cairn had to know when this time came and, in that sense, he or she was an astronomical observer.

Since the recognition of this roofbox at Newgrange similar apertures have been suspected at the passage-grave of Bryn Celli Ddu on Anglesey and at two small chambered tombs alongside Newgrange. When they were finally closed, sealing the burnt bones of the dead inside them, these south-facing mounds may have had gaps left above the rubble that blocked their entrances so that the light of the low midwinter sun could shine down their passages at noon. It is this conjunction of the sky and the dead that is the theme of archaeo-astronomy in the British Isles.

At Maeshowe, the superbly designed passage-grave on Orkney, built around 2700 BC, a similar slit above the blocking slab may have been intended to allow the glow of midwinter sunset to reach into the central chamber. Maeshowe was erected very late in the megalithic tomb tradition and its entrance faced south-west. Often in that final phase entrances opened westwards, quite different from the easterly directions of most neolithic burial places, as though the settings of the sun or moon were becoming more important than their risings. Slieve Gullion, a passage-grave built around 2500 BC on a stupendous mountain in County Armagh, faced south-west, and the scores of wedge-graves in western Ireland, considered to be some of the last

Plate 9. Balnuaran of Clava North-east passage-grave, Inverness. The roof has fallen, exposing the passage and the central chamber. (Photograph: Derek Simpson.)

of the megalithic tombs, had entrances consistently aligned between WNW and SSW.

This re-orientation, which anticipated the sunset ceremonies of the iron age Celts by some 2,500 years, is very obvious in the Clava Cairns of Inverness-shire. Over thirty of these south-west oriented cairns are known, the first perhaps being no earlier than about 3500 BC. Some of them at the head of the Great Glen are passage-graves whose roofed, circular chambers have now collapsed. Others, mostly to the east of the main group and maybe a little later, are ring-cairns with wider but uncovered central spaces. As none of them is more than a few miles from its nearest neighbour it is possible that each was the shrine of an individual family. But, whether passage-grave or ring-cairn, the word 'tomb' is a misnomer. Never more than two burials have been found in any Clava Cairn, far too few for it to have been a graveyard. Even a small family of ten people and their descendants would have suffered some forty deaths during the hundred years that any one of these cairns can reasonably be supposed to have been in use. This, and the scatters of quartz, the careful architecture and the artificial depressions or cupmarks on stones in cardinal positions, all suggest that these places were more than just charnel-houses for the dead.

Nearly all of them have surrounding stone circles whose stones, like the heavy kerbs around the cairns' bases, are graded in height with the tallest in the south-west quadrant. The entrances of the eleven surviving passage-graves also cluster here in a narrow arc between 172 degrees at the SSE and 232 degrees at the south-west (fig. 4). Similar concentrations can be found amongst the famous recumbent stone circles of Scotland, whose architecture is almost identical to that of the Clava Cairns. These stone circles are later than the Clava Cairns and later still are the associated recumbent stone circles of southern Ireland, also with azimuths in the south-west quadrant. If the archaeological links between the three groups are valid then these cairns and rings provide an astonishing example of continuity from 3500 BC or before down to 1000 BC, over two thousand years of an unbroken astronomical tradition.

Alexander Thom, and Somerville before him, noticed that the two passage-graves at Balnuaran of Clava near Inverness faced the midwinter sunset. Since then it has been found that other Clava tombs were planned to look towards the southern moon. A provisional calculation of the declinations of the passage-grave entrances shows a close correspondence with the solar and lunar extremes.

Major southern moonrise (declination -29.1°). Avielochan, - 28.8°;
    Druidtemple, -29.7°; Upper Lagmore, -28.4°.
Major southern moonset (declination -29.1°). Carn Urnan, -29.7°;
    Croftcroy, -29.1°; Kinchyle of Dores, -29.9°.
Midwinter sunset (declination -24.0°). Balnuaran of Clava North-
    east, -24.0°; Balnuaran of Clava South-west, -24.0°.
Minor southern moonset (declination - 18.9°). Carn Daley, -19.0°;
    Corrimony, -18.9°; Dalcross, -18.9°.

Yet although these late megalithic 'tombs' contain alignments that were neater and more accurate than those of the early neolithic mounds there are reasons for doubting that they were observatories for astronomer-priests. The sightlines are very broad. No passage is less than 1 foot 6 inches (457 mm) across nor longer than 29 feet (9 m) so that the narrowest arc of vision from the chamber is 3 degrees wide. Secondly, the lowness of the passage roof in most of the cairns prevented an observer from seeing the skyline. Presumably once the solar or lunar alignment had been defined the sideslabs of the passage were erected along the axis, the corbelled chamber was built, cap-stones were lifted into place and the cairn was piled up over the whole structure. Even if the entrance had been left unblocked the rays of the sun or moon could have reached no more than a few feet down the passage.

If the 'sightline' were for the dead this would have been enough. As at Newgrange and Ballochroy the alignments were symbolic and they would continue to be so even in the vast, open-air monuments of the developed phase that followed.

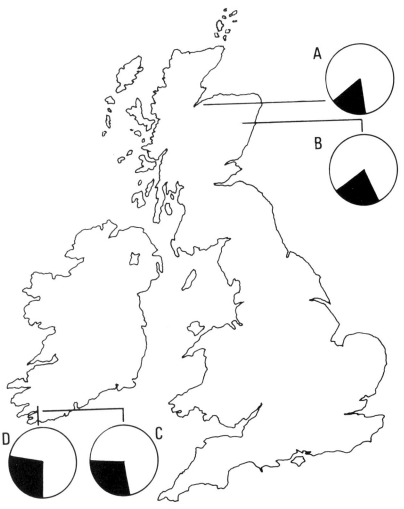

Fig. 4. The azimuths of monuments of the Clava tradition. (A) Clava passage-graves, 172-232 degrees; (B) Scottish recumbent stone circles, 155-235 degrees; (C) Irish recumbent stone circles, 171-294 degrees. Also shown are the Irish wedge-grave azimuths (D), 183-273 degrees.

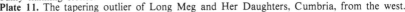

Plate 10. Castlerigg stone circle, Keswick, Cumbria, showing the wide north entrance with its bulky flanking stones.
Plate 11. The tapering outlier of Long Meg and Her Daughters, Cumbria, from the west.

6
The developed phase
3000 to 2000 BC

As society grew more complex and as trading networks expanded it was no longer possible for families to remain self-sufficient, almost isolated from the others, each content with its own place of worship. Communities intermingled and new, larger 'temples' such as Newgrange replaced the old shrines. During the last centuries of the fourth millennium, in the late neolithic period, even more spacious, uncovered enclosures were put up for the crowds of people gathering on the great occasions of the year.

Laborious undertakings such as the construction of Silbury Hill or the quarrying of thousands of tons of chalk from Avebury's ditches reveal how well organised societies now were, with powerful leaders to plan and direct the communal projects. It is probable that as society became more stratified, perhaps with priests or shamans as well as chiefs and craftsmen, so the rituals of summer and winter became more formalised. Performed in the circular henges with their earthen banks or in the novel stone circles of the highlands, these ceremonies necessitated the laying out of accurate alignments in the rings, possibly to mark the times of important gatherings.

As in earlier centuries not every orientation was astronomical. The north-south entrances of henges in Cornwall faced directions where the sun or moon could never have risen or set. Some small henges at Milfield in Northumberland had entrances so arranged that they offered differing views of the horizon. A few miles to their south at Yeavering the opposing entrances of a henge were aligned WNW/ESE towards a 6 foot (1.8 m) high outlying stone and, beyond it, to the conspicuous hill of Ross Castles 10 miles (16 km) away. As long ago as 1892 A. L. Lewis said he knew of at least one hundred examples of stone circles that were aligned on outlying stones and prominent hills, and in 1926 Lily Chitty noticed that three gaps in the Shropshire ring of Black Marsh were in line with hills there. The gap at the SSW was particularly noticeable. 'By placing walking-sticks against [stones] 19 and 20 [Corndon] mountain was exactly framed between them.'

This is in keeping with the belief that natural features could also be the focus of alignments. Yet from the centre stone at Black Marsh the two sides of the entrance have azimuths of 195 degrees and 216 degrees. The declination at their midpoint is -29.8 degrees, very close to the major southern setting of the moon. This suggests that both the hill and the moon may have been targets here, a duality of alignment not unknown in other sites.

At the very beginning of this developed phase people on Salisbury Plain, after years of observations, had the skill to set out two competent sightlines, one to the midsummer sunrise, the other to the major rising of the northern moon. Even today, when the chalk bank is grass-covered and worn down and when several of the outlying stones are missing, this first phase of Stonehenge is still an impressive reminder of the abilities of those early observers.

Sceptics have claimed that weather conditions in the misty British Isles were such that no refined observations would have been practicable and that, in any case, very few sightlines would have been possible in the thickly forested landscapes of prehistory. These opinions seem to be mistaken. Evidence from the almost indestructible husks of pollen and, somewhat unexpectedly, from the shells of light- and warmth-loving snails shows that during this period the climate was milder and drier than it is today, and less cloudy, the cold and pellucid winter skies providing excellent conditions for astronomical observations. It also shows that great tracts of woodland had been cut down by neolithic settlers and that many early stone circles and henges were put up on abandoned farming land in an open, treeless landscape.

Despite the presence of pits containing burnt human bone these first rings had no upstanding structures inside them to hinder the movements of people. They were vast, empty enclosures that impress the modern visitor with the weeks of toil that must have gone into their construction. What is less obvious is the subtlety of their design. To the casual tourist strolling around Castlerigg or Swinside in the Lake District these must seem crude settings of unshaped boulders, romantic perhaps, mysterious in their silence, but rough, unrefined and clumsy. Like the poetry of Donne and Hopkins, however, the harshness is misleading.

The stone circles of Cumbria are indeed composed of unsmoothed boulders but those boulders were aligned with marvellous delicacy on the inconspicuous cardinal points of north, east, south and west. The entrance to Castlerigg is exactly at the north, a direction difficult to establish in the days before the Pole Star. There is a north entrance at Gunnerkeld. Tall stones stand at the west in Elva Plain, at the south at Brats Hill and north at Swinside. Two cumbrous blocks like megalithic loaves squat almost due east-west at Long Meg and Her Daughters and the slight discrepancy in the bearing gives an inkling of how the axis of that spacious ring was laid out.

The builders may have aligned the two stones on the midpoint between the midwinter and midsummer sunsets and with a level skyline this would have resulted in a true east-west axis. Long Meg, however, was erected on a sharpish slope, particularly noticeable to the west, causing the midwinter sun to set a few degrees nearer to the south than it would have done on a lower horizon. Bisecting the distance between the extreme sunsets led to an ENE-WSW alignment, an intriguing glimpse of the working methods of the stone circle builders.

Cardinal alignments have also been noticed at Stonehenge, at Brodgar and Stenness in the Orkneys, Callanish with its straight south-north row of stones, the Druids Temple by Morecambe Bay, Mayburgh near Penrith and in other stone circles and henges, and it seems likely that a majority of them were set out in quadrants whose primary axis was either to the north-south or to the east-west equinoctial directions.

The reasons for such alignments remain contentious. What is even stranger is that the rings frequently had extra sightlines built into them. These can be recognised by the choice of a markedly taller stone or by an entrance or an outlier to act as a foresight. It is these markers that we should study today. The stones should be their own record. It is undiscriminating to accept one convenient notch out of innumerable skyline features unless there is something in the circle that indicates it.

Proof of an alignment demands the existence not only of a target such as the sun or moon but also of a backsight where the observer stood and a foresight to which he looked. In megalithic tombs these might be the chamber and the entrance respectively. In the rings and henges one must assume that the backsight was on the axis and that the foresight was one of the artificial features mentioned earlier.

If such backsights and foresights define an astronomical event one can have some confidence in its significance, especially if it is an event repeated in comparable sites. This is certainly true of the stone circles of Cumbria, where, in addition to the cardinal lines, there are other alignments. They seem to be calendrical.

At the immense ring of Long Meg and Her Daughters there is a line through the entrance to a tapering outlier and to midwinter sunset. At Castlerigg the backsight of the tallest stone is set axially towards the north-west and the azimuth of 307 degrees produces a declination of +24.3 degrees for midsummer sunset. In the other direction the line, with a declination of -16.0 degrees, points to Candlemas sunrise on 1st February. The south-east entrance of Swinside near the Cumbrian coast is aligned on the same February sunrise and so is the ruined entrance of the Girdle Stanes in Dumfries-shire. In Perthshire Croft Moraig's entrance looks to the equinoctial sunrise.

A February alignment is not as improbable as one might think. Alexander Thom suggested that prehistoric people divided the year into sixteen equal periods. This brilliant deduction may be a slight over-refinement of a simpler calendar. If, instead, one took every other one of Thom's 'months', the eight declinations correspond very closely to those of iron age feast days three thousand years later. Later still, Christianity adopted and adapted these when the Church was struggling to overcome heathen customs. It is ironical that celebrants of All Souls Day should unknowingly be perpetuating a festival of the dead that began five thousand years ago in a pagan stone circle.

Table 3 lists Thom's eight even-numbered epochs, omitting the eight intervening odd numbers. It also gives their azimuths for latitude 55 degrees, and the various festivals, prehistoric and Christian, that are associated with them.

Table 3. Eight of Alexander Thom's 'Megalithic Months' (azimuths for latitude 55 degrees.)

			azimuths (55°)		festivals	
epoch	*'month'*	*declination*	*sunrise*	*sunset*	*prehistoric*	*Christian*
2	8th May	+16.6°	60°	300°	Beltane	Whitsun?
4	21st June	+23.9°	45°	315°	Midsummer solstice	
6	9th August	+16.7°	60°	300°	Lughnasa	Lammas; Harvest festival
8	23rd September	+0.4°	90°	270°	Autumn equinox	
10	6th November	−16.3°	119°	241°	Samain	All Souls; All Saints; Martinmas
12	21st December	−23.9°	135°	225°	Midwinter solstice	Christmas
14	5th February	−16.2°	119°	241°	Imbolc	St Brigid's; Candlemas
16	23rd March	+0.4°	90°	270°	Vernal equinox	

It is interesting to see how many alignments in the early stone circles correspond to the times of the Celtic festivals of Beltane, Lughnasa, Samain and Imbolc. The association is not confined to Cumbria. But whereas those sightlines usually looked towards a sunrise the circles of western Britain more often had sunset orientations.

At Ballynoe in County Down, a ring similar to those in the Lake District, the entrance faced WSW. Two henges at Llandegai near Bangor had WSW entrances. So did the sacrificial Druid's Circle on a headland overlooking Conway Bay and the Stripple Stones circle-henge on Bodmin Moor. Here, in 1905, against a fallen off-centre stone the excavator, Gray, found four deep postholes where the builders may have been attempting to establish an accurate backsight.

Cornish stone circles such as the attractive Trippet Stones often have their tallest stone at the WSW. Near Land's End, in the haunted ring of Boscawen-Un with its leaning internal pillar the only quartz stone is at the WSW. And in southern Ireland two heavy blocks arranged like a gunsight opposite the entrance to the Grange circle-henge in County Limerick were thought by Windle to stand in line with the early November sunset of Samain when the Celtic year came to its end and the dead rose from their graves.

Beltany Tops, a circle in County Donegal associated with the May assembly of Beltane, also has a Samain alignment. From the backsight of a stone covered in cupmarks an axial sightline points to the foresight of the ring's tallest stone at the WSW in line with the sunsets of both Samain in November and Imbolc in February. With more research others of these 'Celtic' calendrical orientations might be detected in henges and stone circles, showing how neolithic and bronze age people held rituals at times of the year more customarily thought to be iron age in origin. If, as some claim, the druids had a bronze age origin there is no reason why the festivals linked with them should not be just as old.

At Stonehenge, the monument most popularly inhabited by druids, Hawkins has suggested that more sightlines were added when the thick circle of sarsen stones was erected. Built around 2100 BC, this heavy ring enclosed a horseshoe-shaped setting of five separate stone archways, each made of two enormous standing stones with a lintel across them. This horseshoe of trilithons ('three-stones') is claimed to possess a complete set of sightlines to midwinter and midsummer sunrises and sunsets and to the southern moonrises and northern moonsets. They are very coarse, some of them several degrees wide, and they remain controversial, but if they are genuine prehistoric alignments their purpose presumably was calendrical.

Plate 12. Easter Aquorthies stone circle, Aberdeenshire. The massive recumbent stone and its tall flankers are seen from the east inside the ring. (Photograph: Derek Simpson.)

This is not true of all sightlines. In some circles alignments were defined by grading the heights of the stones as the builders of the Clava Cairns had done. Several rings in southern Britain are graded but it is a feature best seen in the recumbent stone circles of north-east Scotland. The cremated bone, quartz, cupmarks and inner ring-cairns of these sites reflect their Clava associations but the recumbent stone, a huge block lying between the two tallest stones of the ring, is not to be seen in any Clava Cairn. Yet the southerly azimuths of these great stones, between 155 and 235 degrees, occupying an arc almost identical to the Clava passage-grave entrances, leave no doubt that they belong to the same tradition.

The recumbents, it seems, were aligned on the southern moon. Some rings face the extreme rising of the moon in the south, more face its setting and still others look to where the moon would have been high in the southern sky. The normal situation for a recumbent stone circle was on a hillside. From here the moon on the far-off horizon would be neatly framed as it passed between the hornlike stones that flanked the recumbent. It was an accurate but broad alignment. The diameter of an average circle here is about 66 feet (20 m) so that with a recumbent stone 12 feet (3.7 m) long an observer would have had an arc of vision over 10 degrees wide. It would take the moon about an hour to pass across such an arc and this may have been what the users of the ring wanted in their ceremonies. Had they been making scientific observations, however, they surely would have created a sharper sightline.

Scottish recumbent stone circles continued to be built until about 2200 BC, well over a thousand years after the first Clava Cairn. It is a length of time that emphasises how long-lived the Clava tradition was along the coasts of the Moray Firth and in north-east Scotland, a longevity possibly caused by the comparative isolation of the followers of that cult.

Their beliefs were not those of the south. The recumbent stone circles, just as closely grouped together as the Clava Cairns, were family monuments unlike the wide and open communal enclosures elsewhere in Britain in this developed phase. In the recumbent stone circles the lunar alignments brought the moon into association with the dead and the 'sightlines' had a purpose different from the calendrical lines of Cumbria. But in all the regions the circles were well built and the alignments were carefully laid out.

It was a fastidiousness that did not endure. As the megalithic tradition slowly declined the astronomy also suffered neglect.

7
The local phase
2000 to 1250 BC

With the fertile lowlands becoming over-populated, the early bronze age saw widespread settlement in areas that had remained almost uninhabited throughout the neolithic. For a few centuries the climate permitted the cultivation of thinner upland soils, and during the early years of the second millennium BC regions such as Dartmoor, the Yorkshire Moors, the Cheviots and the Boggeragh mountains of southern Ireland were farmed by energetic and resourceful families. It was they who erected many of the bleak rings and rows of stones that still stand on today's deserted moors.

In a landscape of long steep hillsides, the valleys between them divided by leaping streams and rivers, the farmsteads of these settlers must often have been solitary places. There were few large communities and in the hill country the new ritual centres were small. There was no need of large enclosures, nor did the few men and women have the resources to build them. Instead, they put up inexact and scaled-down versions of the great circles and henges, the constricted four-poster rectangles of Perthshire, the cairn-circles of Dartmoor, the mixture of henge and megalithic ring to be seen in the unspectacular embanked stone circles of the Peak District.

They were for few people. Far into Dartmoor, rings such as Down Tor were only a fifth the size of Scorhill and other early circles at the edge of the moor. A Scottish four-poster with its central burial pit was no bigger than a modern sitting room. Even Callanish could accommodate no more than forty people comfortably.

There are so many late rings in the British Isles that it seems every little settlement had its own, whether of stone or earth or timber, the posts long since having rotted, leaving no trace above ground of where they stood. A few people could have built any of them. In these rows and circles the stones were not gross. Even a pillar 6 feet (1.8 m) high and 3 feet (900 mm) thick weighed less than 4 tons and could have been pulled upright by fifteen men and women without strain, three or four families working together. It is, moreover, seldom that stones as big as this were put up in these late stone settings.

With rings as small as Dooish in County Tyrone, 15 feet (4.6 m) across, or the 18 feet (5.5 m) diameter of Sandy Road, Scone, built around 1500 BC, the stones were too close together for any good sightline to be taken across the axis. Even the other monuments thought to be of this period are no more promising. There are single stones, some horseshoes of standing stones in northern Scotland and there are rows of stones on moorland fringes in many parts of the British Isles. Some of them are very late. An alignment at Maughansilly in County Kerry was erected around 1600 BC and, nearby, at Cashelkeelty a row alongside a tiny five-stone ring was put up not much earlier than 1200 BC.

To the archaeo-astronomer these final megaliths are nightmares. In some the sightlines are too short for precision. Some lack foresights and so have to be rejected. Some were built inexpertly. Others were not astronomical. Unless a whole group can be found with repeated sightlines it is probably wiser to disregard these lonely stones and meandering rows and, instead, concentrate upon the more rewarding structures. The reasons are clear.

One stone by itself mocks understanding. It might have marked a trackway. It might be the remnant of a wrecked row or circle. It may have been moved. Even if from it a notch on the horizon coincides nicely with an astronomical event there is no certainty that the stone itself was ever a backsight. Lacking a foresight, the stone's date and function remain unknown. The 16 feet 4 inches (5 m) high pillar at Beacharra demonstrates the problem. Thom thought it might indicate the major northern moonset but Clive Ruggles observed that this thin slab was not oriented 'anywhere near' the necessary azimuth of 326 degrees. More probably its south-north axis was related to the chambered tomb a few yards away.

Even several stones in line are questionable. The low stones of the Eleven Shearers in Roxburgh, a row over 460 feet (140 m) long, were believed to point to the equinoctial sunrise. Yet if the row had been designed as a sighting device one wonders why the builders laid it out over a low crest so that one end could not be seen from the other. It is so irregular that it may be the decayed remains of a field boundary associated with the late bronze age earthwork of Hownam Rings close by.

Other rows are just as enigmatic. Parc y Meirw, eight stones in a line 130 feet (40 m) long near Fishguard in Dyfed, has been claimed as 'undoubtedly lunar' because its axis lies in the direction of the minor northern moonset. For this alignment to work one would have to be able to see a mountainous foresight near Mount Leinster in Eire 91 miles (146 km) away, so distant that because of atmospheric refraction it may never have been visible.

The Devil's Arrows in Yorkshire raise another objection. These three towering, striated pillars stand in a long line whose declinations to NNW and SSE are of little astronomical interest but whose axis is repeated in the entrances of the henges at Thornborough, Cana and Hutton Moor just to the north and in the Roman road, in the river Swale and even the railway line as it passes the alarmingly named Leys Burn. It was not astronomy but the lie of the land that decided these alignments and attempts to impose astronomical inter-pretations upon them would almost certainly be misleading.

Much caution is required when examining late megalithic sites. Even if the rings and rows did contain sightlines these are anything but clearcut because the astronomical mechanism is so clumsy. Whereas a fine alignment can be obtained from two thin poles 50 feet (15 m) apart, the same accuracy is not possible with a pair of rough stones only 9 feet (2.7 m) from each other, as is the case at Newtyle near Dunkeld in Perthshire. These coarse, lumpish blocks of schist are set with the taller to the north-west. The builders may have intend-ed a midsummer sunset alignment but the unshaped boulders do not provide a clean azimuth of 310 degrees. Instead there is a blur of possible sightlines anywhere between 290 and 330 degrees with a declination range from + 14.0 to + 32.2 degrees, taking in both the major and minor settings of the northern moon as well as the sunset but without a convincingly unequivocal alignment anywhere.

At the strange complex of circles, rows and cairns at Beaghmore in County Tyrone, constructed some time after 1900 BC, the rows that wander erratically north-eastwards from the rings have been found to be aligned, badly, on either midsummer sunrise or on the major rising of the northern moon. The correlations are poor. For the sun the declinations vary from +22.4 to +26.6 degrees instead of focusing on +23.9 degrees, and for the moon, +26.1 to +31.4 degrees instead of +29.1 degrees. The results were so crude that Dr Archie Thom wondered whether the erectors were mere beginners learning about the moon's movements. In so late a period they were probably peasant farmers struggling with something beyond their ability.

Constantly in these late sites human bone is found. There were cairns between the circles at Beaghmore. In the Peak District, at Barbrook II, built around 1850 BC, John Barnatt thought that Candlemas and Lammas sunlines and southern moonlines were built into the axial settings of the ring and he produced a good plan to demonstrate this. The builders may have intended the astronomy but they certainly intended the cist with its cupmarked slab, the pyre, and the cremation under the cairn which they put up inside the embanked circle. On Salisbury Plain the little girl interred at Woodhenge lay in a grave facing the midsummer sunrise, buried there by people whose

Plate 13. The Beaker burial on Roundway Down, Wiltshire. The man lies on his left side, head to the north, facing east.

beliefs were not the same as ours because their way of life was not the same.

Death was never far from their imagination and the sun and moon were never far from their vision of death. Even in their graves there were orientations. Frequently in the highlands a body or its cremated remains was placed in a slab-lined cist and these cists followed the same tradition of preferred alignments as the megalithic tombs before them. On Dartmoor the cists, over eighty of them, had a predominantly northwest-southeast disposition. In northern Britain cists with burials accompanied by thick-lugged food-vessels were often built with their long sides set north-south.

Even corpses laid in ordinary graves were arranged according to the custom of the region. In Yorkshire burials with fine beaker pots had men with their heads to the east, women with heads to the west, both facing south. More commonly, both on the continental mainland and in Britain the makers of such pottery preferred to put the bodies in graves that were dug north-south, men's heads to the north, women's to the south, both looking to the east.

A young man buried in a wooden coffin at the centre of a ditched circle near Stanton Harcourt in Oxfordshire, a quiver of arrows at his hip, a beaker by his head, lay crouched with hands on his shoulders, head at the north, looking eastwards through the timber side of his coffin, through the gravel of the grave pit, towards the sunrise. This was never an alignment for the living but it does show how the living followed the solar and lunar traditions when rites were performed for the dead.

These were the realities of astronomical practice. They reveal the intimate, mystical transpositions of sun, moon, life and death in the minds of the same people whose rows and rings of stones frustrate our understanding. A pair of stones at Orwell in Perthshire had human bone in one of the stoneholes, put there before the stone was raised. The cist at Ballochroy was aligned, like the row there, northeast-southwest towards the midwinter sunset and it is facts such as these that tell us most clearly that the orientations were symbolic rather than scientific, for obsequies rather than observations.

This belief is confirmed by recumbent stone circles in Scotland and Ireland and by associated monuments. Stones deliberately laid flat, as the recumbents were, seem consistently astronomical. The spiral-carved entrance stone at Newgrange lay across the line of the midwinter sunrise. Martin Brennan believes that a similar stone at Knowth passage-grave was oriented on equinoctial sunrise. The Scottish recumbent stone circles and their Clava Cairn forebears were aligned on important solar and lunar positions.

This is true of related sites also. Croft Moraig in Perthshire, a circle whose stones are graded in height like those of Aberdeenshire, has an eastern entrance. Much less conspicuous is the overgrown stone lying prostrate on the south-west perimeter, its surface pitted with cup-marks (fig. 5). From the centre of the ring the stone has an azimuth of 200 degrees and a declination of −29.2 degrees, that of the major southern moonset.

The cairn at Kintraw in Argyll has the same orientation. This site with its cisted cremation has, like Ballochroy, been acclaimed as a precise solar observatory because a standing stone near it is almost in line with midwinter sunset. The sunset cannot actually be seen from the cairn, which, in any case, is not quite in the right place, but the discovery of a possible viewing platform cut into the suicidally precipitous hillside behind the cairn has excited some if not all archaeo-astronomers.

Kintraw, however, has the disregarded but notable feature of an 'entrance' at its SSW with a long, supine stone in front of it. The entrance consisted of two standing stones flanking an upright slab that resembled the blocking stone to a passage. Kintraw has no passage, only thousands of cairnstones covering the spot where a central post had stood. So neatly fashioned is this 'entrance' and so eye-catching before cairnstones tumbled over it that it must have been

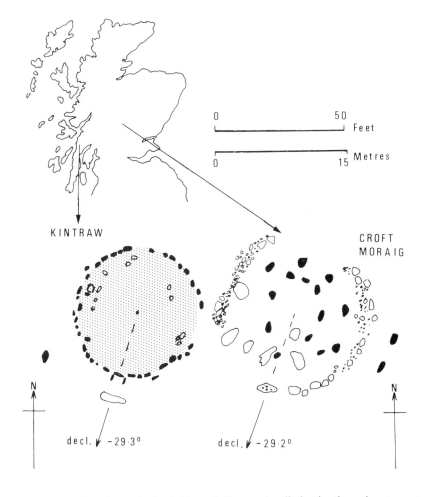

Fig. 5. Plans of Croft Moraig, Perthshire, and Kintraw, Argyll, showing the supine stones at their SSW.

important to the builders. Useless for the living, it provided a 'doorway' for the dead. Astronomically it is interesting.

The people had propped up the post on Kintraw's grassy terrace. Then, using it as a pivot, they set out a circle of graded kerbstones as a precinct for their rites. With the post as a backsight they put up the stones of the false entrance, aligning it SSW towards a nearby steep ridge. This was the place, with a declination of −29.3 degrees, where the southern moon set at its extreme and this, surely, was what the people had sighted towards. Then, having deposited some burnt bones in a cist, they piled the mass of cairnstones over everything just as other people did at Ballochroy some 30 miles (48 km) to the south, entombing the dead and obscuring the alignment.

Such associations between megaliths, astronomy and death are commonplace but in this local phase the smallness of the rings and the shortness of many rows meant that good sightlines were rare. It is unlikely that families wanted much more than a general orientation and imprecision may not have mattered. This is suggested by the Irish recumbent stone circles.

Between north-east Scotland and south-west Ireland there are sites such as Croft Moraig and Kintraw whose likeness to the Scottish circles hints at connections between them, but it is hundreds of miles to the south that rings most like those of Aberdeenshire exist, spread along the coasts of Cork and Kerry. They are not replicas. They are smaller, their tallest stones stand opposite the recumbent rather than alongside it and if they have a ring-cairn it is not inside the circle but some distance from it. Further inland in the Boggeragh mountains a similar transformation occurred for here the little five-stone rings only differ from the Perthshire four-posters in their retention of a recumbent slab. These Irish recumbents are believed to be later than their Scottish counterparts and radiocarbon dates from Cashelkeelty's five-stone ring support this, showing that the stones were put up between 1200 BC and 900 BC, some 2,500 years after the earliest of the Clava Cairns.

It is the astronomy that confirms the Clava-Aberdeen-Munster connection. The azimuths in south-west Ireland of 170 to 294 degrees cover the same arc as those of the Scottish chambered tombs and stone circles with the addition of an extension to the WNW. Nineteen of the thirty-two known declinations, those with azimuths between 171 and 235 degrees, are lunar although the short diameters cause wide arcs of vision. The five-stone ring of Rylane, only 12 feet (3.7 m) across but with a recumbent stone nearly 7 feet (2.1 m) long, offers an arc from 200 to 230 degrees and although the central declination of -30 degrees is in line with the major setting of the

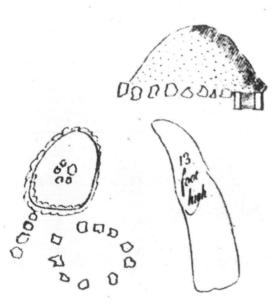

13.
foot high

southern moon the lunar alignment is more like a panoramic window than an astronomical peephole.

The Irish rings here that do not conform to the lunar pattern are good examples of intermixing of traditions and act as warnings against facile interpretations. These untypical circles such as Carrigagulla and Derreenataggart lie inland where chambered cairns known as wedge-graves had been built by settlers long before the arrival of the stone circle people. The entrances to these unusual tombs faced between SSW and WNW and it is likely that the incoming circle builders, mingling with the natives, accepted the older tradition, aligning their own rings not on the moon but on the sunsets of February and November.

Yet, whether the moon or the sun, the astronomy was fused with death. Burnt human bone lay in the wedge-graves. And at the centre of the Cashelkeelty ring was a slab-covered pit and in it were the cremated remains of a young adult. From the vague beginnings in the neolithic long graves down to these last little stones three thousand years later the associations were the same.

Even with the abandonment of the uplands as the climate worsened and when the megalithic tradition had faded some of the customs endured. The occasions of the Celtic festivals demanded the keeping of a calendar. And, in the iron age, temples and shrines at Heathrow, Brigstock, Winchester and Danebury faced eastwards. At South Cadbury the porched shrine also faced east and outside its verandah pits with offerings of sacrificed animals lay in line with the equinoctial sunrise. Thousands of years earlier people had buried an ox outside the east-facing entrance of the passage-grave of Bryn Celli Ddu on Anglesey, a tomb that may have had a solar roofbox.

Visitors to these ancient places today often sense the mysteries contained within the stones but it is our ignorance, not the forgotten powers of a psychic world, that causes our feeling of loss. From the first neolithic tomb to the last iron age temple the stones were not mysteries to the people who raised them.

8
The future

Archaeo-astronomy is no longer regarded as an activity of the lunatic fringe. It has become a respectable study. It now needs to become a respectable discipline. It is no longer acceptable to go to a single site, find a promising skyline feature and assert that this proves an astronomical purpose. As this book has shown, there are so many other possibilities and the astronomical 'evidence' is so susceptible to misinterpretation that more rigorous methods are needed.

From the early chambered tombs, through the henges and stone circles, down to the last grass-grown rings of posts and stones there stretched three thousand years of prehistory. During that period the climate changed, the ways of life changed, society and rituals changed. Every region was geographically different. To expect a passage-grave in an Irish valley, a stone circle on a Cumbrian hillside and a stone row on the moors of Caithness to have a similar astronomical function is naive. Instead, groups should be studied, groups in the same region, of the same architecture and of the same period.

In the primitive phase there are the Cotswold-Severn tombs of southern England with such splendid sites as West Kennet, Stoney Littleton and Hetty Pegler's Tump, none of which has been properly studied astronomically. There are the Clyde tombs of south-west Scotland and the Camster tombs of the north. In the developed phase one could study the magnificent Cumbrian stone circles to see how widespread the interest in cardinal points was. In the local phase there are the remarkable multiple rows of Caithness and Sutherland, Mid Clyth, Dirlot and Learable Hill among them, or the pairs of standing stones in Perthshire, the taller to the west, possibly in line with the setting of the sun or moon.

There is also the possibility that in particular regions traditions continued over the long period from the primitive to the local phase. As one instance, around the Preseli mountains of Wales there are chambered tombs, a cist-circle at Cerrig-y-Gof, the stone circle of Gors Fawr and some standing stones. Such a regional group would be worth examination. If similar orientations occur in many of the monuments it could show how steadfast and conservative beliefs and customs could be in prehistoric times.

When the henges and barrows and megalithic sites were abandoned

Plate 16. The multiple rows of stones at Mid Clyth, Caithness. Thom has suggested that these were laid out to indicate the rising positions of the northern and southern moon. (Photograph: Crown Copyright, Ancient Monuments Record, Edinburgh.)

it was slowly forgotten that the sun and moon had been vital to the people who had built them. Only a legend or two prevented an entire darkness spreading over them. With persistence and care it may be possible for us to bring back some of the light.

9
Sites to visit

For detailed information about sites with possible astronomical alignments the reader should refer to the books by D. C. Heggie and A. Thom listed in the bibliography. The sites suggested on this page are still in good enough condition for the visitor to inspect the sightlines and judge for himself how likely they are.

Those marked with an asterisk are in state care and are open to the public during the official hours. The others are on private land and permission to visit them should be sought from the landowner.

Stone circles

Beaghmore, County Tyrone.*	H	685842
Beltany Tops, County Donegal	C	254003
Brodgar, Orkneys*	HY	294132
Callanish, Isle of Lewis*	NB	213330
Castlerigg, Cumbria*	NY	292236
Croft Moraig, Perthshire	NN	797472
Drombeg, County Cork*	W	247352
Loanhead of Daviot, Aberdeen*	NJ	747288
Long Meg and Her Daughters, Cumbria*	NY	571373
Stonehenge, Wiltshire*	SU	123422

Stone rows

Ballochroy, Argyll	NR	730524
Mid Clyth, Caithness	ND	294384
Parc y Meirw, Dyfed	SM	999359

Other sites

Balnuaran of Clava, Inverness*	NH	757444
Kilmartin Stones, Argyll	NR	827977
Kintraw, Argyll	NM	830050
Newgrange, County Meath*	O	007727

10
Glossary

Alignment: three or more points deliberately placed in a straight line.

Archaeo-astronomy: the study of ancient astronomy. Once known as astro-archaeology.

Azimuth: a compass-bearing taken from true north. An azimuth of 90 degrees is due east.

Barrow: a round or long prehistoric burial mound of earth or chalk.

Beaker: a finely made, flat-bottomed pot of the late neolithic and early bronze ages in the British Isles.

Bronze age: the period of bronze tools and weapons in the British Isles from about 2400 BC to 1000 BC.

Cairn: As for *barrow* but composed of small stones.

Candlemas: the Christian feast of the Virgin Mary on 2nd February.

Cardinal point: the four directions of north, south, east and west.

Cist: a prehistoric grave lined with slabs and covered by a capstone.

Corbelled: walls whose courses are stepped inwards like a beehive.

Declination: the angular distance of a celestial body from the celestial equator. The equator has a declination of 0 degrees, the North Pole one of 90 degrees north. Declination is the only accurate means of expressing the position of the sun or moon at any particular time and is calculated from the combination of latitude, azimuth and horizon height (see page 20).

Elongation: the angular distance of a celestial body from the sun.

Equinox: the times when daylight and darkness are of equal length around 21st March (vernal equinox) and 23rd September (autumnal equinox). At such times the sun rises due east and sets due west.

Five-stone ring: a small bronze age ring of four upright stones and one recumbent stone. Mainly found in south-west Ireland.

Four-poster: a small bronze age ring of four upright stones at the corners of a rough rectangle. Mainly found in central Scotland.

Gallery-grave: once the term for a neolithic long mound with a gallery of large stones, sometimes with side-chambers.

Henge: a late neolithic or early bronze age circular or oval enclosure with earth or chalk banks, often with an internal ditch and one or more entrances.

Kerbstone: one of a continuous ring of heavy stones around the base of a cairn or barrow.

Lammas: 1st August, once the Christian harvest festival.

Martinmas: 11th November, the Christian feast of St Martin of Tours.

Megalithic: *mega* = big; *lith* = stone. Composed of large and heavy stones. Stonehenge is a megalithic monument.

Meridian: a line through the North and South Poles. At the meridian the sun is at its highest in the sky, due south at noon.

Mica schist: a slaty rock composed of regular beddings of quartz and mica. These laminations permit the stone to split easily into thin slabs.

Neolithic: new stone age. When tools and weapons were of stone, flint, bone or wood. From about 4750 to 2400 BC in the British Isles.

Orientation: the direction of an object from a given position. Sometimes used in place of *alignment* but this is careless usage. All objects will have an orientation whether or not anything is aligned on them.

Orrery: a model showing the movements of the planets around the sun.

Outlier: a standing stone outside a prehistoric monument such as a stone circle.

Parallax: the apparent movement of an object when seen from different positions. The effect of parallax can easily be seen by looking at a nearby object with first the left and then the right eye.

Passage-grave: a megalithic tomb with a long passage leading to a chamber near the centre of the covering mound. Found mainly in the west of the British Isles.

Quadrant: one of the four quarters of a circle which has been divided by north-south and east-west lines.

Recumbent stone circle: a Scottish bronze age circle of standing stones that rise in height towards a large prostrate block. Slightly different types of recumbent stone circle occur in south-west Ireland.

Refraction: light rays from a celestial object are bent as they pass into and through the atmosphere and so the object appears higher than it really is. This effect is known as refraction.

Ring-cairn: a low cairn, usually surrounded by kerbstones, with a central, uncovered space in which cremations are often found. Neolithic and bronze age.

Row: a line of three or more standing stones.

Shaman: a medicine-man or priest-doctor who was supposed to have power over the spirits of the natural world.

Solstice: *sol* = sun, *stice* = stand. The sun's 'standstill'. The extreme positions of the sun at midsummer and midwinter when its eastern risings and western settings appear to take place in the same position on the horizon for three or four days in succession.

Wedge-grave: an Irish megalithic tomb consisting of an oval or D-shaped cairn with a wedge-shaped gallery that faces between south and west.

Wessex: Wiltshire and surrounding counties on the chalklands of southern England which were densely populated in prehistoric times.

11
Further reading

Astronomical background
Hadingham, E. *Early Man and the Cosmos*. Heinemann, 1983.
Heggie, D. C. *Megalithic Science*. Thames and Hudson, 1981.
Krupp, E. C. *Echoes of the Ancient Skies*. Harper and Row, 1983.
Michell, J. *A Little History of Astro-Archaeology*. Thames and Hudson, second enlarged edition, 1989.
Wood, J. E. *Sun, Moon and Standing Stones*. Oxford University Press, 1978.

Practical work
Duffett-Smith, P. *Practical Astronomy with your Calculator*. Cambridge University Press, 1979.
Hogg, A. H. A. *Surveying for Archaeologists and Other Fieldworkers*. Croom Helm, 1980.

Current work
Brennan, M. *The Stars and the Stones*. Thames and Hudson, 1983.
Heggie, D. C. (editor). *Archaeoastronomy in the Old World*. Cambridge University Press, 1982.
MacKie, E. W. *Science and Society in Prehistoric Britain*. Elek, 1977.
Petrie, W. M. F. *Stonehenge: Plans, Description and Theories. With an update by G. S. Hawkins*. Histories and Mysteries of Man Ltd, 1989.
Ruggles, C. L. N. *Megalithic Astronomy: A New Archaeological and Statistical Study of 300 Western Scottish Sites*. BAR 123, Oxford, 1984.
Ruggles, C. L. N. (editor). *Records in Stone. Papers in Memory of Alexander Thom*. Cambridge University Press, 1988.
Ruggles, C. L. N., and Burl, H. A. W. 'A New Study of the Aberdeenshire Recumbent Stone Circles, 2: Interpretation'. *Archaeoastronomy*, 8 (1985), S25-S60.
Ruggles, C. L. N. and Whittle, A. W. R. (editors). *Astronomy and Society in Britain during the Period 4000-1500 BC*. BAR 88, 1981.
Thom, A. *Megalithic Sites in Britain*. Oxford University Press, 1967.
Thom, A. *Megalithic Lunar Observatories*. Oxford University Press, 1971.

Thom, A. and A. S. *Megalithic Remains in Britain and Brittany.* Oxford University Press, 1978.

Prehistoric sites
Ashbee, P. *The Earthen Long Barrow in Britain.* Second edition, Geo Books, 1984.
Burl, A. *Rites of the Gods.* Dent, 1981.
Burl, A. 'Stone Circles : the Welsh Problem'. *Council for British Archaeology Report* 35 (1985), Appendix A, 72-82.
Burl, A. 'The Sun, the Moon and Megaliths'. *Ulster Journal of Archaeology,* 50 (1987), 7-21.
Burl, A. *The Stonehenge People.* J. M. Dent, 1987.
Henshall, A. S. *The Chambered Tombs of Scotland, I, II.* Edinburgh University Press, 1963, 1972.
Thom, A. and A. S. and Burl, A. *Megalithic Rings: Plans and Data for 229 Sites.* BAR 81, 1980.
Thom, A. and A. S., and Burl, A. *Stone Rows and Standing Stones: Britain, Ireland and Brittany, I, II.* BAR 560, Oxford, 1990.

Journals
As well as occasional articles in archaeological magazines such as *Antiquity* there is the journal *Archaeoastronomy*, the supplement to the *Journal for the History of Astronomy.* This is an annual publication. The learned papers in it contain much technical data and it may be over-detailed for some readers. Those interested should write to: Science History Publications Ltd, Halfpenny Furze, Mill Lane, Chalfont St Giles, Buckinghamshire, HP8 4NR.

Pioneers
Readers wanting references to the work of early investigators such as Lewis, Lockyer and Somerville should see the books listed in D. C. Heggie's *Megalithic Science.*

Index

Page numbers in italic refer to illustrations